HOW GREAT IS OUR GOD

— PIANO LEVEL —
LATE ELEMENTARY/EARLY INTERMEDIATE
(HLSPL LEVEL 3-4)

ISBN-13: 978-1-4234-2548-9
ISBN-10: 1-4234-2548-0

HAL•LEONARD®
CORPORATION

7777 W. BLUEMOUND RD. P.O. BOX 13819 MILWAUKEE, WI 53213

Visit Hal Leonard Online at
www.halleonard.com
Visit Phillip at
www.phillipkeveren.com

PREFACE

Learning to play the piano is an exciting adventure. One of the greatest rewards is playing songs that have special meaning to you. Hearing that favorite tune spring from the piano through one's own fingers is a unique joy.

As you develop the gift of music that God has given you, it is a privilege to worship through songs that were written expressly for His pleasure. This folio is a collection of some of the finest praise and worship songs. My hope is that you will enjoy learning them, and then share your gift of music with friends and family. Volunteer to play an offertory or solo in your church. Your church family will be blessed by your offering.

How great is our God!
Phillip Keveren

BIOGRAPHY

Phillip Keveren, a multi-talented keyboard artist and composer, has composed original works in a variety of genres from piano solo to symphonic orchestra. Mr. Keveren gives frequent concerts and workshops for teachers and their students in the United States, Canada, Europe, and Asia. Mr. Keveren holds a B.M. in composition from California State University Northridge and a M.M. in composition from the University of Southern California.

CONTENTS

ABOVE ALL

Words and Music by PAUL BALOCHE
and LENNY LeBLANC
Arranged by Phillip Keveren

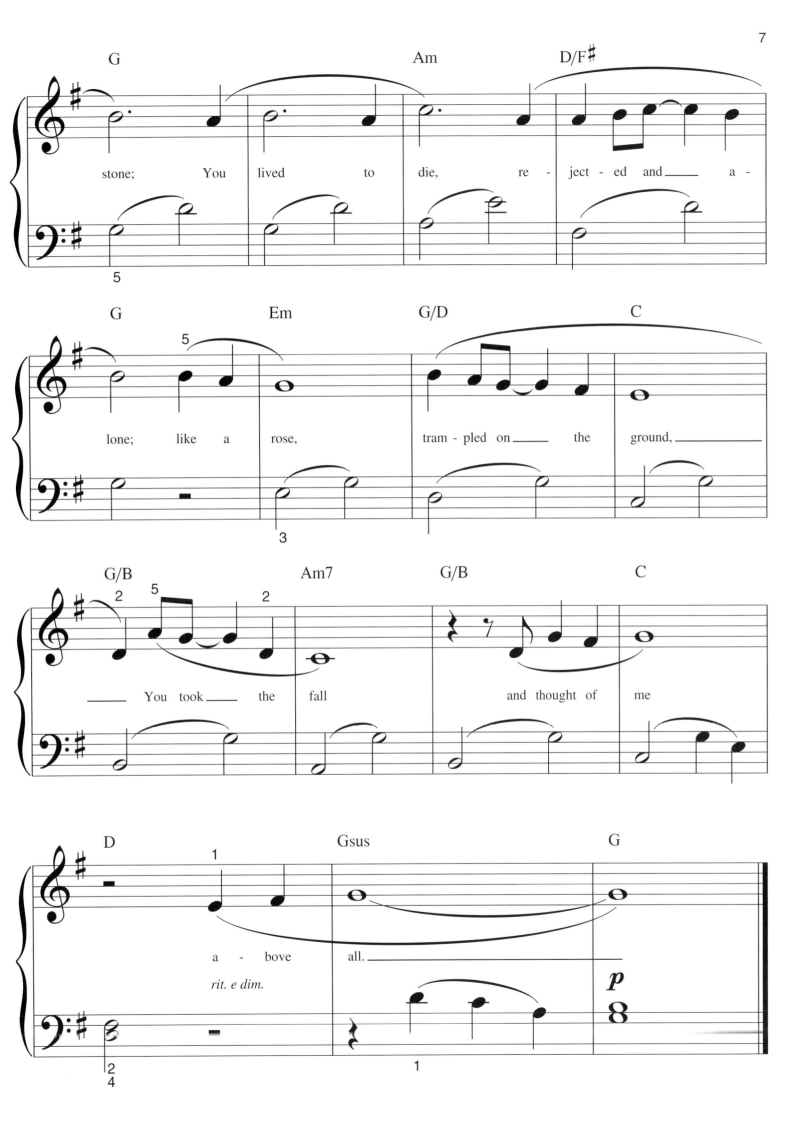

AWESOME GOD

Words and Music by
RICH MULLINS
Arranged by Phillip Keveren

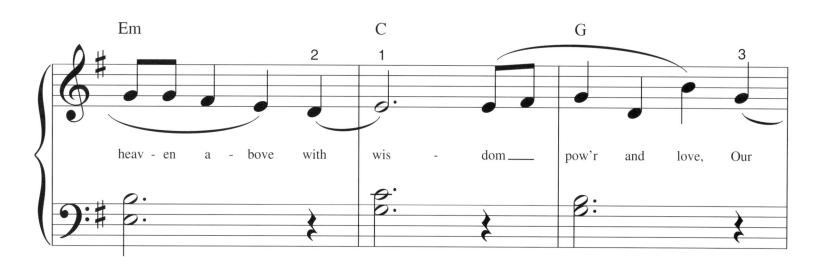

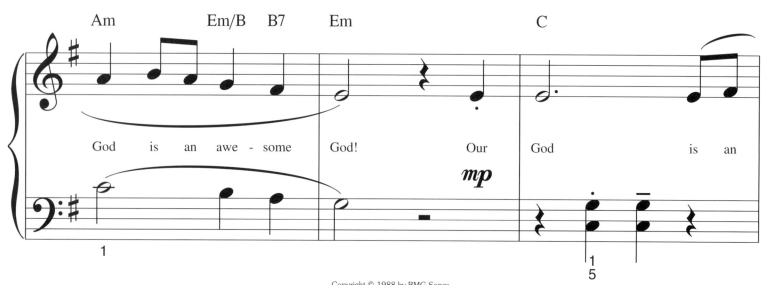

BLESSED BE YOUR NAME

Words and Music by MATT REDMAN
and BETH REDMAN
Arranged by Phillip Keveren

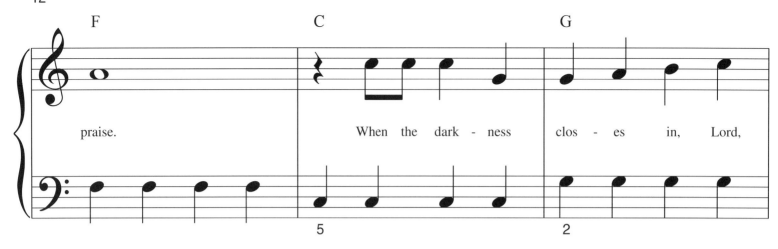

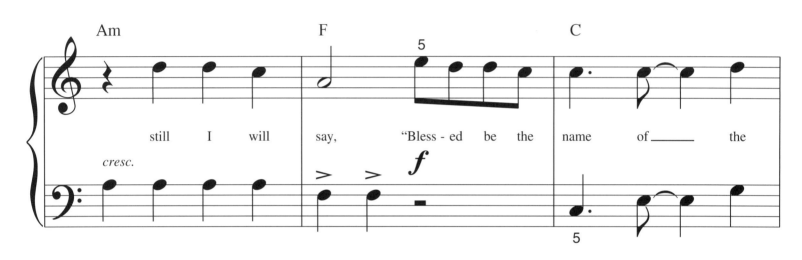

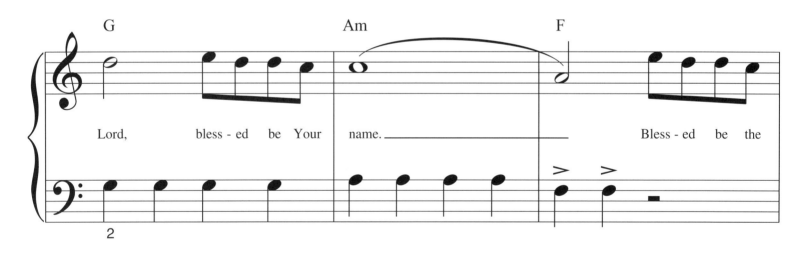

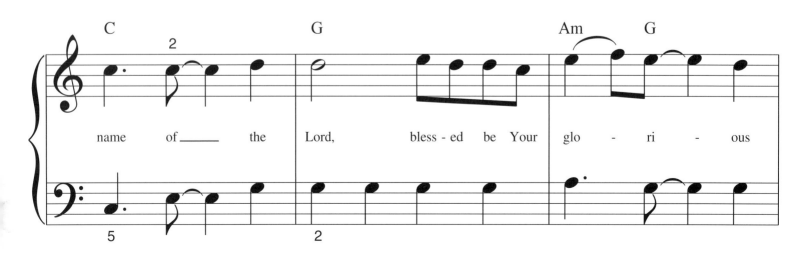

DAYS OF ELIJAH

Words and Music by
ROBIN MARK
Arranged by Phillip Keveren

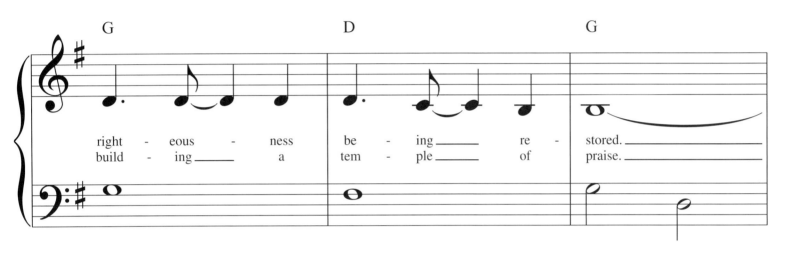

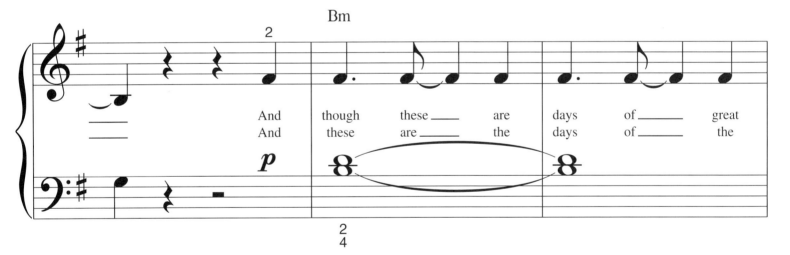

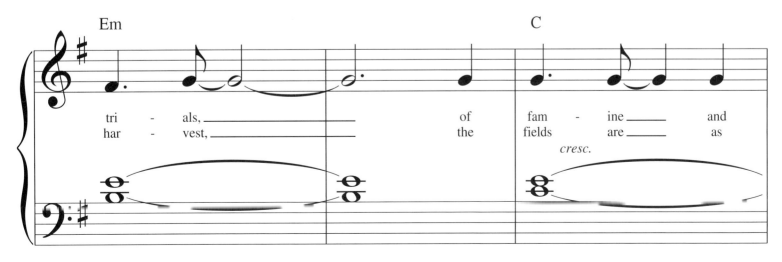

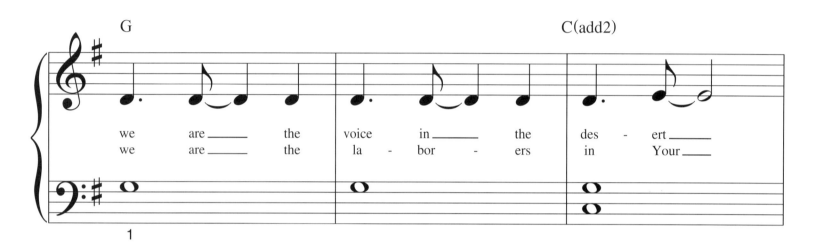

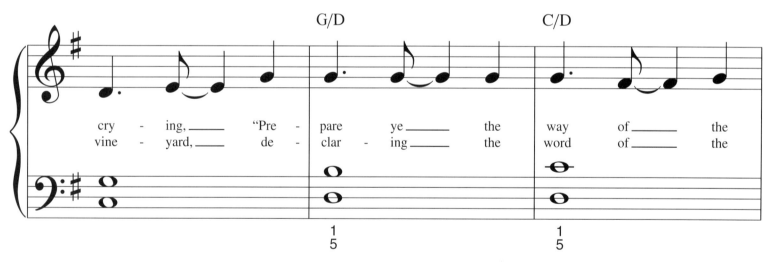

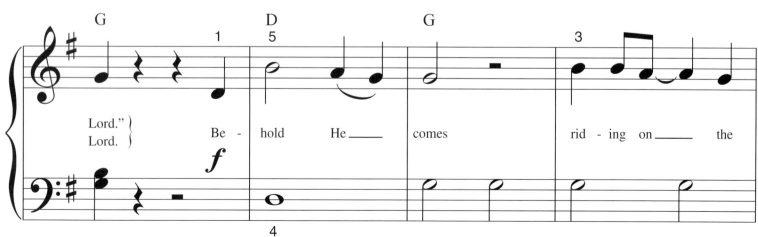

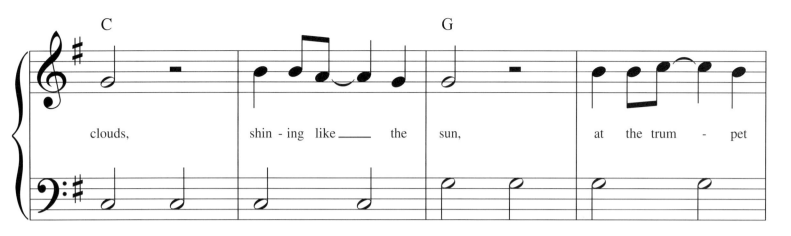

clouds,   shin - ing like ____ the   sun,   at   the trum - pet

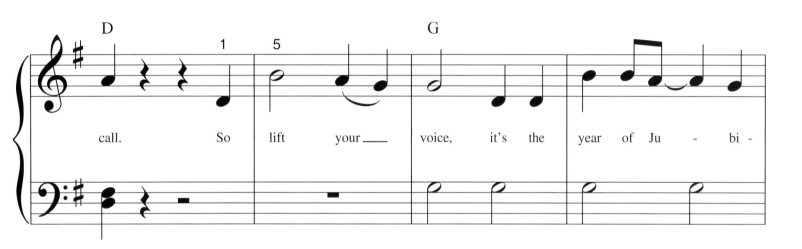

call.   So   lift   your ____ voice,   it's   the   year of Ju - bi -

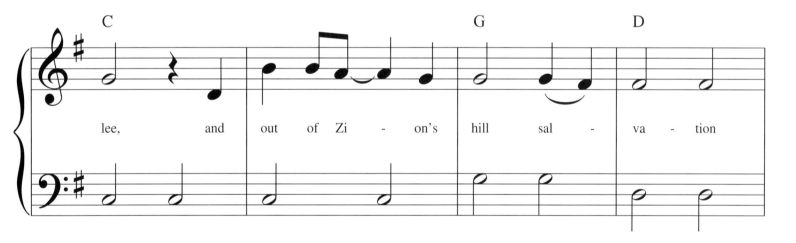

lee,   and   out of Zi - on's   hill   sal - va - tion

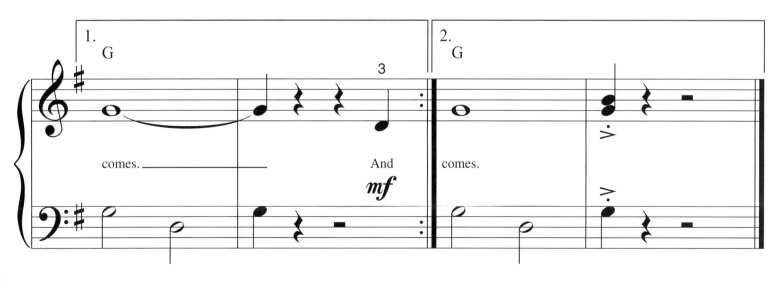

comes. _____   And   comes.

FOREVER

Words and Music by
CHRIS TOMLIN
Arranged by Phillip Keveren

GIVE THANKS

Words and Music by
HENRY SMITH
Arranged by Phillip Keveren

GOD OF WONDERS

Words and Music by MARC BYRD
and STEVE HINDALONG
Arranged by Phillip Keveren

With praise (♩ = 80)

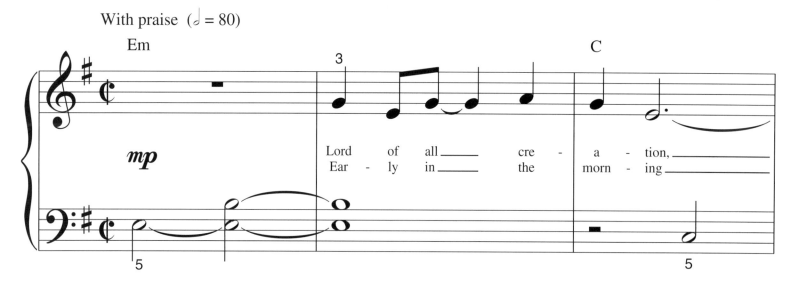

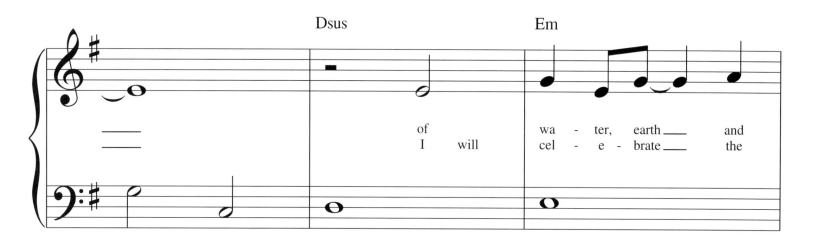

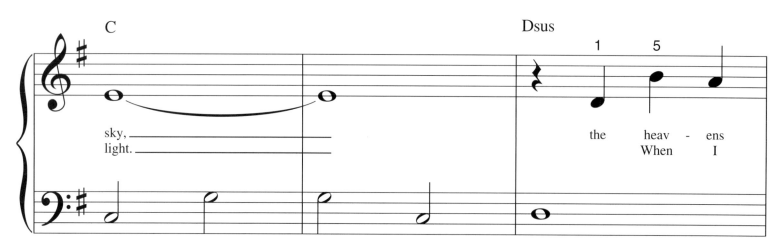

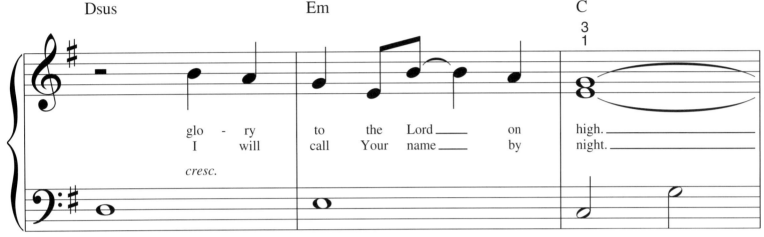

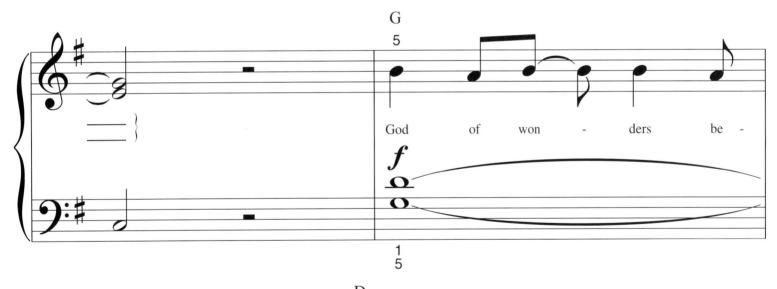

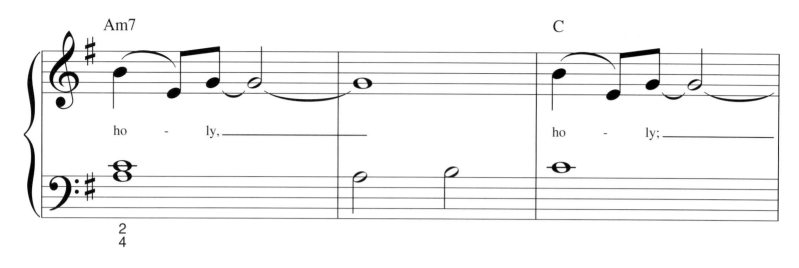

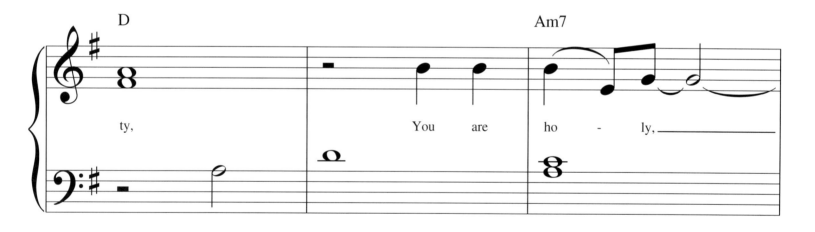

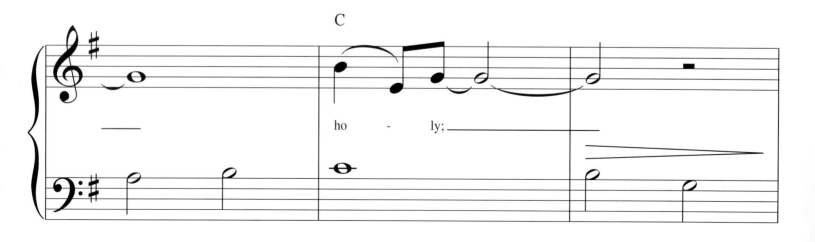

HERE I AM TO WORSHIP

Words and Music by
TIM HUGHES
Arranged by Phillip Keveren

Tenderly (♩=76)

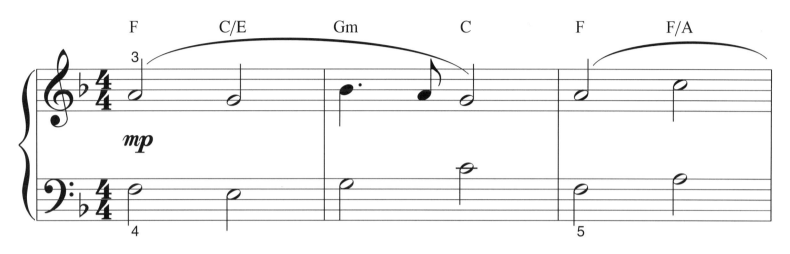

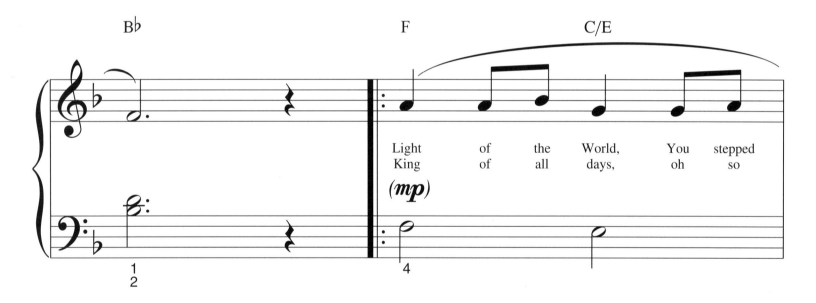

Light of the World, You stepped
King of all days, oh so

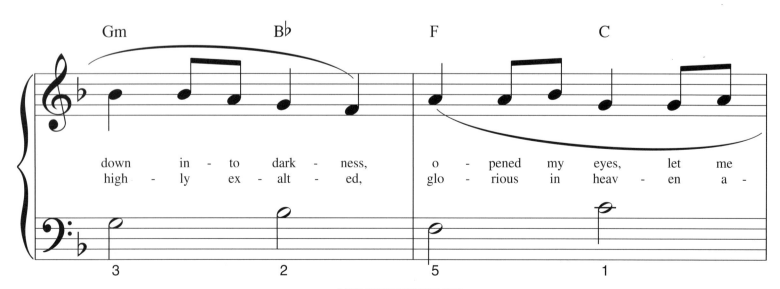

down in - to dark - ness,   o - pened my eyes, let me
high - ly ex - alt - ed,   glo - rious in heav - en a -

HOW GREAT IS OUR GOD

Words and Music by CHRIS TOMLIN,
JESSE REEVES and ED CASH
Arranged by Phillip Keveren

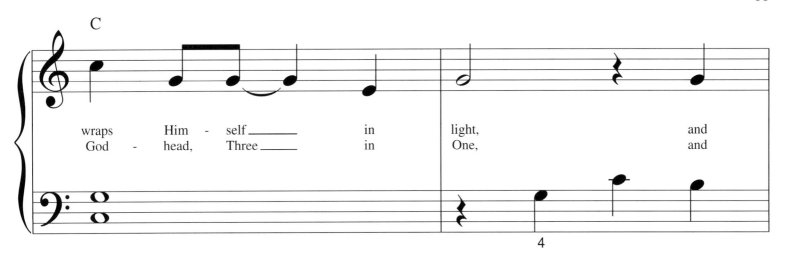

wraps Him - self _____ in light, and
God - head, Three _____ in One, and

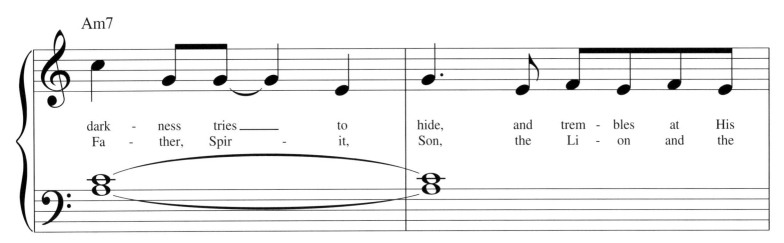

dark - ness tries _____ to hide, and trem - bles at His
Fa - ther, Spir - it, Son, the Li - on and the

voice, trem - bles at His voice. } How
Lamb, Li - on and the Lamb. }

great _____ is our God! Sing with me: How

Am7

great _____ is our God! And all will see how

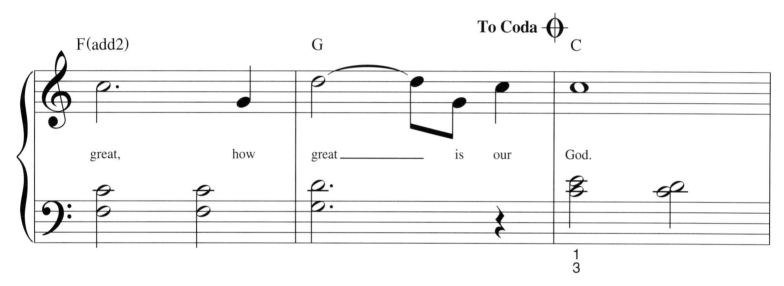

To Coda ⊕

F(add2)   G   C

great, how great _____ is our God.

1.   2.

And   'Cause You're the   Name a - bove ___ all

mf

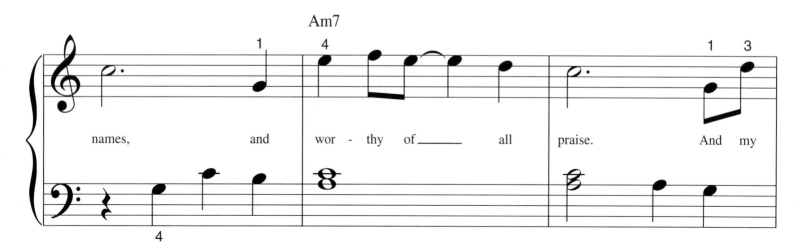

Am7

names,   and   wor - thy of ___ all   praise.   And my

OPEN THE EYES OF MY HEART

Words and Music by
PAUL BALOCHE
Arranged by Phillip Keveren

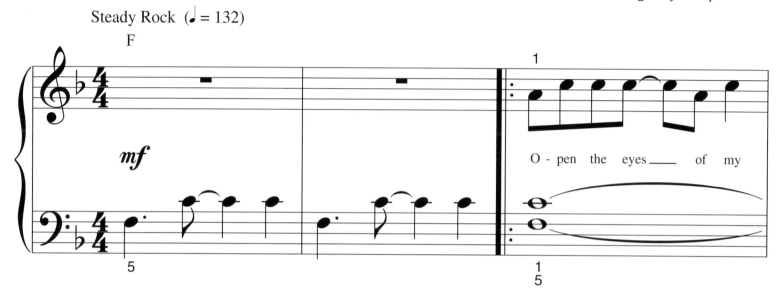

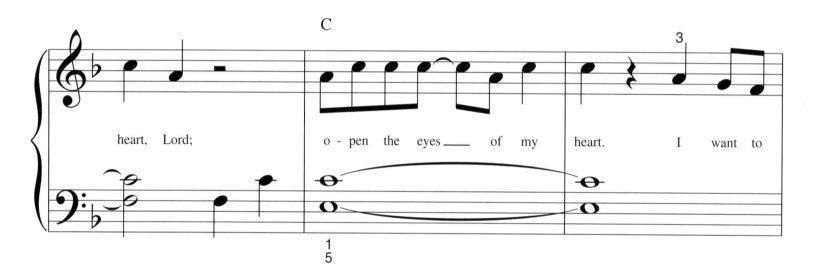

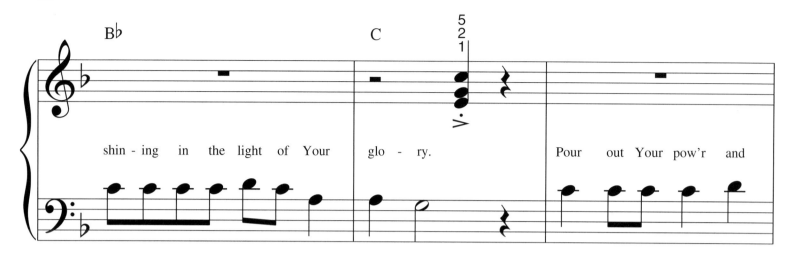

shin-ing in the light of Your glo-ry. Pour out Your pow'r and

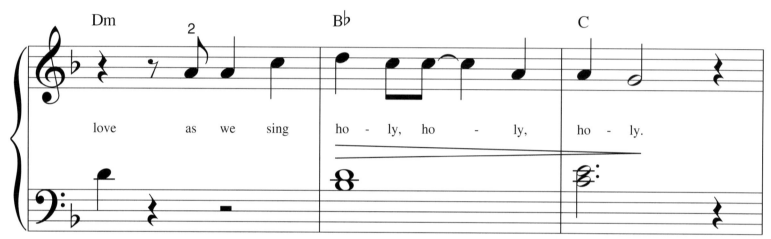

love as we sing ho-ly, ho-ly, ho-ly.

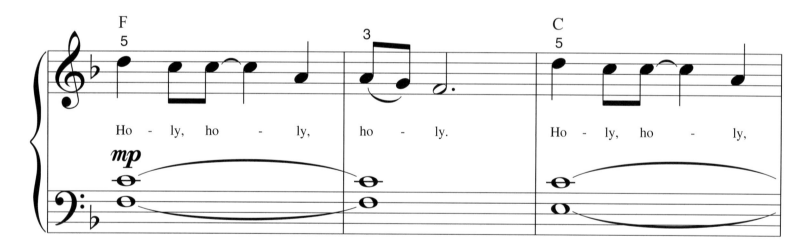

Ho-ly, ho-ly, ho-ly. Ho-ly, ho-ly,

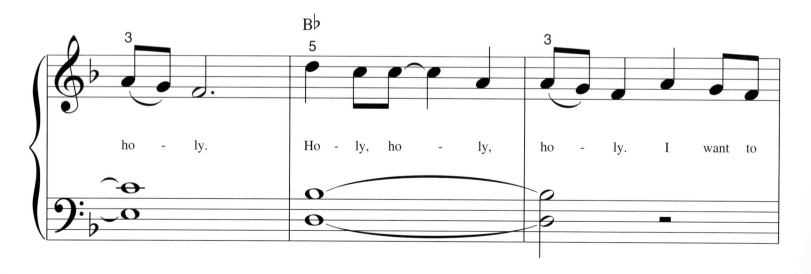

ho-ly. Ho-ly, ho-ly, ho-ly. I want to

THE POTTER'S HAND

Words and Music by
DARLENE ZSCHECH
Arranged by Phillip Keveren

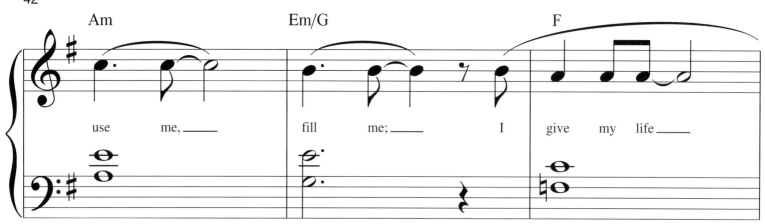

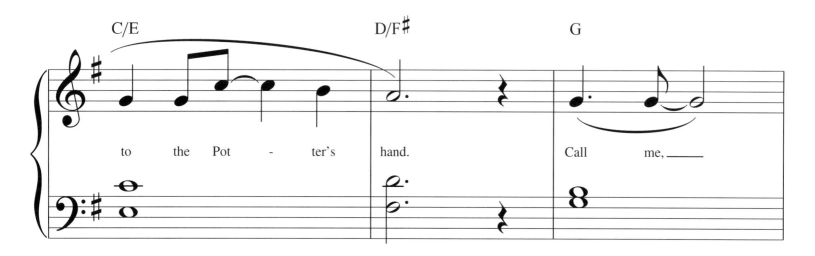

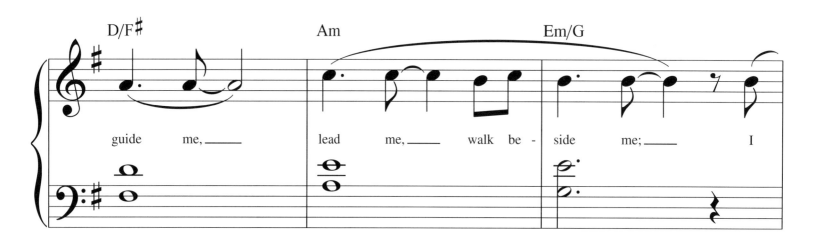

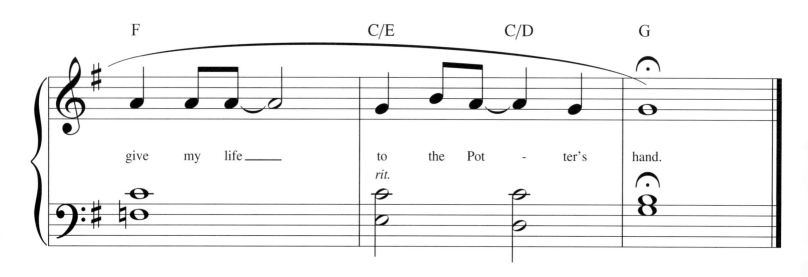

SHOUT TO THE LORD

Words and Music by
DARLENE ZSCHECH
Arranged by Phillip Keveren

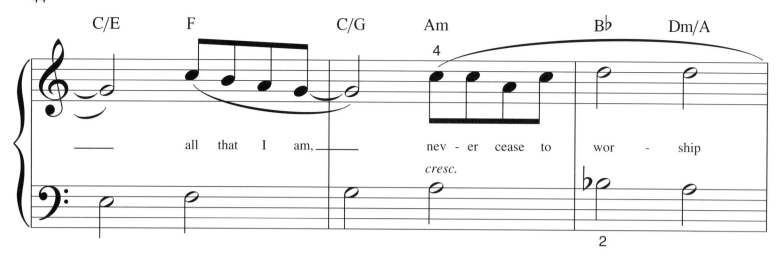

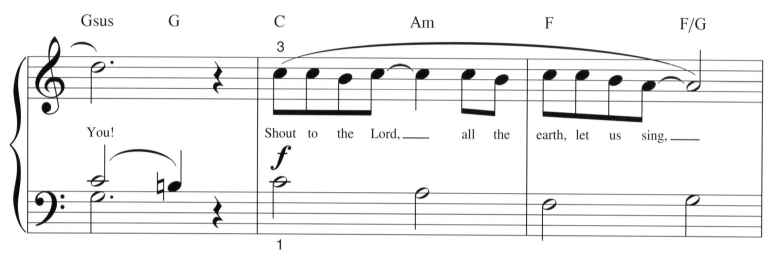

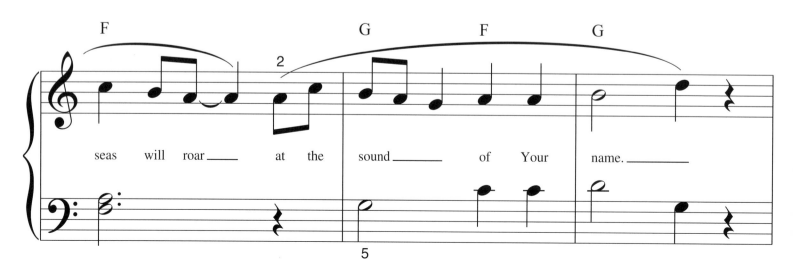

THERE IS A REDEEMER

Words and Music by
MELODY GREEN
Arranged by Phillip Keveren

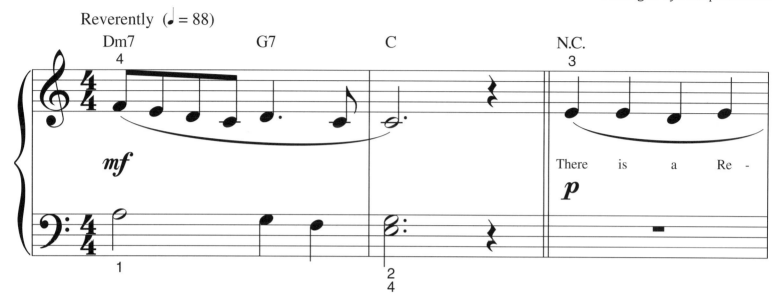

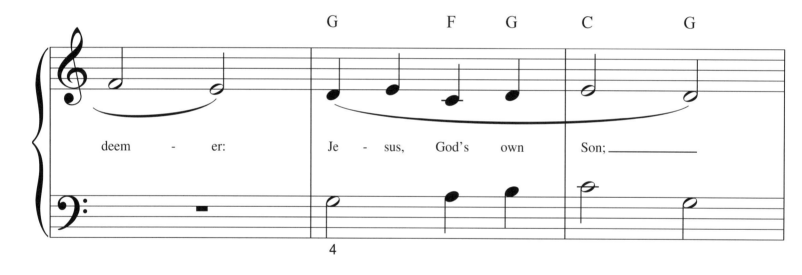

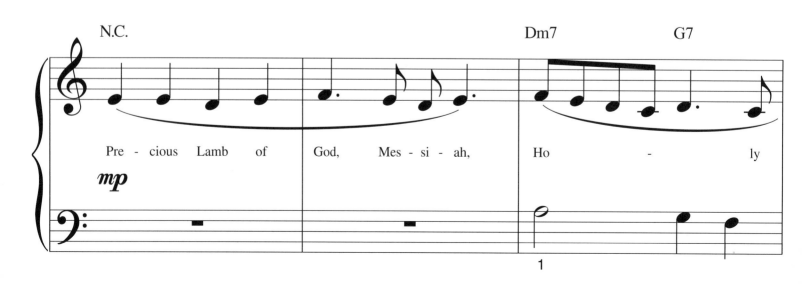

THERE IS NONE LIKE YOU

Words and Music by
LENNY LeBLANC
Arranged by Phillip Keveren

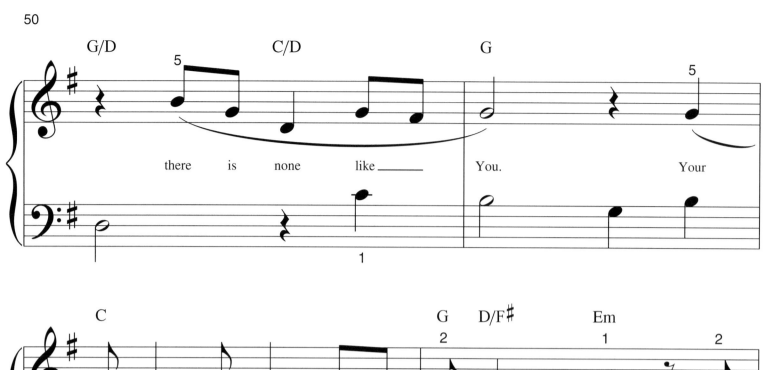

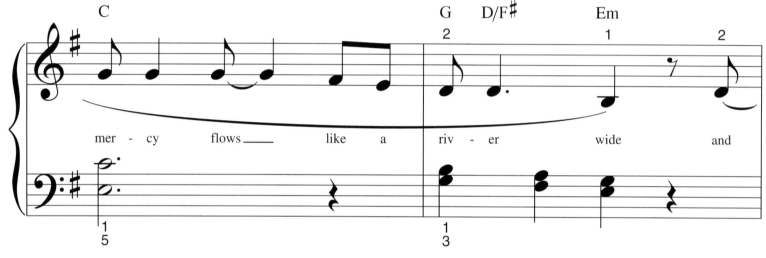

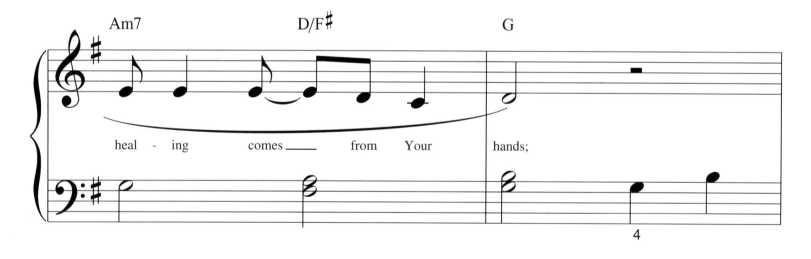

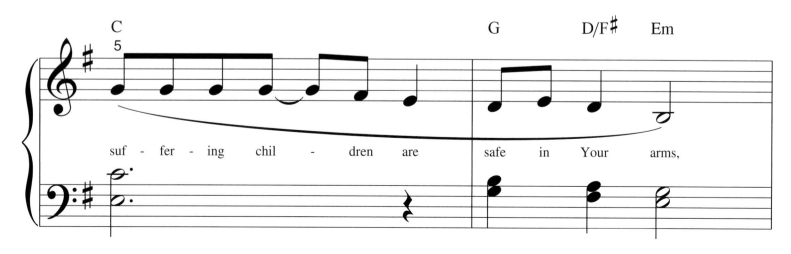

WE FALL DOWN

Words and Music by
CHRIS TOMLIN
Arranged by Phillip Keveren

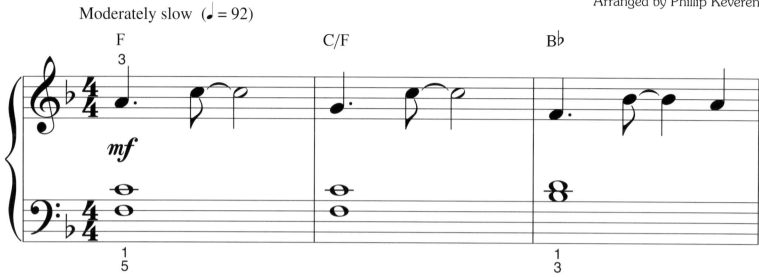

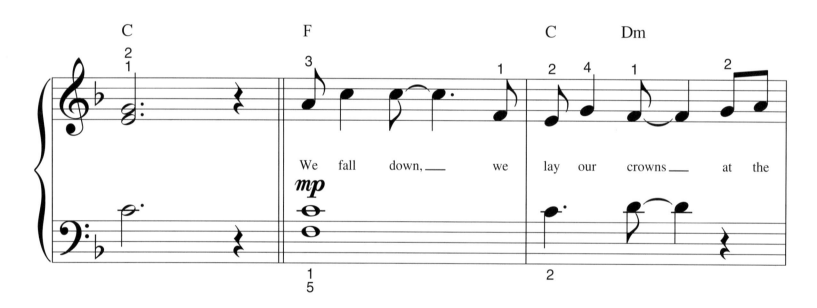

We fall down,___ we lay our crowns___ at the

feet of Je - sus,_____ the great - ness of_____

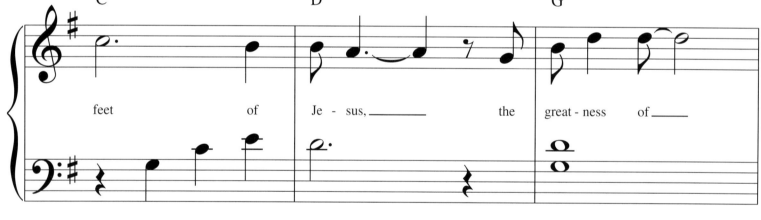
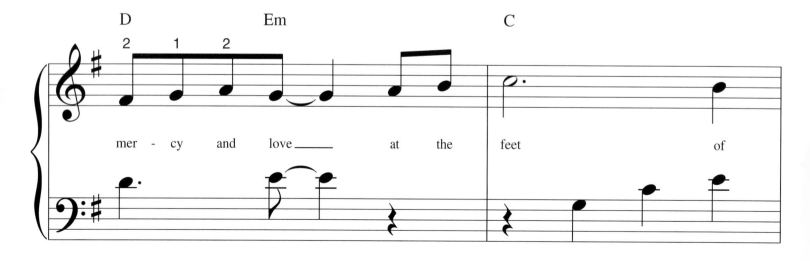

THE PHILLIP KEVEREN SERIES

PIANO SOLO —
Late Intermediate/Early Advanced Level

ABOVE ALL
00311024 ....$11.95

THE BEATLES
00306412 ....$12.95

BROADWAY'S BEST
00310669 ....$12.95

A CELTIC CHRISTMAS
00310629 ....$10.95

THE CELTIC COLLECTION
00310549 ....$12.95

CINEMA CLASSICS
00310607 ....$12.95

CLASSIC WEDDING SONGS
00311101 ....$10.95

CLASSICAL FOLK
00311292 ....$10.95

CLASSICAL JAZZ
00311083 ....$12.95

CONTEMPORARY WEDDING SONGS
00311103 ....$12.95

GREAT STANDARDS
00311157 ....$12.95

THE HYMN COLLECTION
00311071 ....$10.95

HYMN MEDLEYS
00311349 ....$10.95

HYMNS WITH A TOUCH OF JAZZ
00311249 ....$10.95

I COULD SING OF YOUR LOVE FOREVER
00310905 ....$12.95

JINGLE JAZZ
00310762 ....$12.95

LET FREEDOM RING!
00310839 ....$9.95

ANDREW LLOYD WEBBER
00313227 ....$14.95

MOTOWN HITS
00311295 ....$12.95

RICHARD RODGERS CLASSICS
00310755 ....$12.95

SHOUT TO THE LORD!
00310699 ....$12.95

SMOOTH JAZZ
00311158 ....$12.95

EASY PIANO —
Early Intermediate/Intermediate Level

AFRICAN-AMERICAN SPIRITUALS
00310610 ....$9.95

CELTIC DREAMS
00310973 ....$10.95

CHRISTMAS POPS
00311126 ....$12.95

A CLASSICAL CHRISTMAS
00310769 ....$10.95

CLASSICAL MOVIE THEMES
00310975 ....$10.95

EARLY ROCK 'N' ROLL
00311093 ....$10.95

GOSPEL TREASURES
00310805 ....$11.95

THE VINCE GUARALDI COLLECTION
00306821 ....$12.95

IMMORTAL HYMNS
00310798 ....$10.95

JAZZ STANDARDS
00311294 ....$12.95

LOVE SONGS
00310744 ....$10.95

POP BALLADS
00220036 ....$12.95

RAGTIME CLASSICS
00311293 ....$10.95

SWEET LAND OF LIBERTY
00310840 ....$9.95

TIMELESS PRAISE
00310712 ....$12.95

TV THEMES
00311086 ....$10.95

21 GREAT CLASSICS
00310717 ....$11.95

BIG-NOTE PIANO —
Late Elementary/Early Intermediate Level

BELOVED HYMNS
00311067 ....$12.95

CHILDREN'S FAVORITE MOVIE SONGS
00310838 ....$10.95

CHRISTMAS MUSIC
00311247 ....$10.95

CONTEMPORARY HITS
00310907 ....$12.95

HOLIDAY FAVORITES
00311335 ....$12.95

HOW GREAT IS OUR GOD
00311402 ....$12.95

JOY TO THE WORLD
00310888 ....$10.95

THE NUTCRACKER
00310908 ....$8.95

THIS IS YOUR TIME
00310956 ....$10.95

BEGINNING PIANO SOLOS —
Elementary/Late Elementary Level

AWESOME GOD
00311202 ....$10.95

CHRISTIAN CHILDREN'S FAVORITES
00310837 ....$10.95

CHRISTMAS FAVORITES
00311246 ....$10.95

CHRISTMAS TIME IS HERE
00311334 ....$10.95

CHRISTMAS TRADITIONS
00311117 ....$9.95

EASY HYMNS
00311250 ....$10.95

KIDS' FAVORITES
00310822 ....$10.95

MOVIE MUSIC
00311213 ....$10.95

PIANO DUET —
Early Intermediate Level

CLASSICAL THEME DUETS
00311350 ....$9.95

PIANO DUET —
Late Intermediate Level

PRAISE & WORSHIP DUETS
00311203 ....$11.95

FOR MORE INFORMATION, SEE YOUR LOCAL MUSIC DEALER,
OR WRITE TO:

HAL•LEONARD®
CORPORATION
7777 W. BLUEMOUND RD. P.O. BOX 13819 MILWAUKEE, WI 53213

Visit Hal Leonard online at **www.halleonard.com**

Prices, contents, and availability
subject to change without notice.

0207